FELICIA CARTRIGHT

AND THE
UNCUT DIAMOND

Felicia   Joan

FELICIA CARTRIGHT

AND THE
UNCUT DIAMOND

BERNARD PALMER

ANEKO
PRESS

Cover Artwork: Adobe Firefly
Editor: Charlene Miskimen

Aneko Press Youth

www.anekopress.com

Aneko Press, Life Sentence Publishing, and our logos are trademarks of
Life Sentence Publishing, Inc.
203 E. Birch Street
P.O. Box 652
Abbotsford, WI 54405

JUVENILE FICTION / Religious / Christian / Action & Adventure

Paperback ISBN: 979-8-88936-288-3

eBook ISBN: 979-8-88936-289-0

10 9 8 7 6 5 4 3 2 1

Available where books are sold

CONTENTS

CHAPTER 1

A TRIP TO FRANCE

The sun had dropped out of the cloud-dusted sky and was slipping below the horizon. Only a thin, red slice remained. It cast long, tenuous shadows across the lane and the neat, square patches the French called fields. Shadows that molded trees and hedge fences into strange, fantastic shapes and wrapped the countryside in gloom.

Felicia Cartright and her companion, Joan Bailey, paused uncertainly and glanced around as they reached the lane. The little peasant hut, set back from the road a hundred paces or so, looked more like an old painting than a place where people lived. And the hush that was everywhere added to the illusion.

"Are you sure this is the house?" Joan asked.

Felicia nodded. "It's got to be. Great-Uncle Don gave us such careful directions before we left that we couldn't possibly miss it."

Joan pursed her lips and looked around. The shadows were everywhere, creeping stealthily through the silent fields and pastures. Quaint old-fashioned huts and barns blurred in the growing darkness and began to lose form and substance. Joan cleared her throat uneasily. A shudder tingled up her spine.

"I'm not sure that I like this," she said, laughing uneasily. "It gives me the creeps."

Felicia brushed a blond curl from her eyes and shifted her backpack from one hand to the other. A Frenchman plodding along the road turned to stare at them. They were so obviously American. Their clothes, their hair, their very manner shouted it. American, and quite young.

So young, in fact, that Miss Duncan, Dean of Women at Wellington School for Girls, had been most reluctant to let them leave the group to carry out the errand for Felicia's Great-Uncle Don Morgan. It was only when she showed Miss Duncan the letter of introduction from Uncle Don to the Duvalls that she agreed for them to miss the lecture and go out to the country that afternoon.

It all began when a wealthy alumna left a large sum to the school for "education by travel" scholarships.

"I want four deserving students to travel, properly chaperoned by Miss Duncan, of course," she had told the board of directors, "to the countries of Europe."

Felicia's grades were in the upper ten percent of her class, and her list of extracurricular activities were enough to make her first choice for any award, but it was a surprise to everyone that Joan was even considered. As a matter of fact, although the girls were never aware of it, Mrs. Waldo herself was the one who insisted that Joan be included.

"She is a lovely girl," Miss Duncan informed the donor crisply, "especially since she became a Christian, but I am sorry to say that she is not among our better students. I'm quite sure that we can find someone who would be a much better representative of the Wellington ideal."

But Mrs. Waldo was firm. "I want Joan Bailey," she insisted.

"She is only an average student. The only thing she is above average in is popularity."

Mrs. Waldo drew herself up to her full height and set her mouth firmly. "Then make the award for her popularity. Her mother was very kind to me when I first came to Wellington. Now I have a chance to do something nice for her daughter."

And so, Joan Bailey and Felicia Cartright had been selected, along with two others, to make the trip.

"I can't understand it," Joan said, shaking her dark hair. "With all the A students here at Wellington, why did they choose me?"

"Because you're one of the sweetest, nicest girls here at school," an underclassman said loyally.

Joan laughed.

"You'd just as well stow that kind of talk. It isn't

going to get you any help from me on your English themes."

"We know better than to flatter you expecting help on anything related to studies," someone else said, laughing. "Now if it were Felicia–"

Felicia Cartright felt the color come up in her cheeks, and she smiled self-consciously.

"It won't do any good for you to ask her to help you," Joan countered. "I'm her best friend, and she even makes me do all my own studying."

Felicia shook her head. Joan was always talking that way. Making jokes about wanting to do her studies for her. Of course, she didn't actually mean it. Especially after she accepted Christ as her Savior.

"Will you send us a postcard from Paris?" one of the girls asked breathlessly.

"If you're good girls, we might even bring you some of that luscious French perfume."

"Would you?" they chorused.

They were still talking when Linda Hodges and Dorothy Craig came bursting into the room.

"You'll never be able to guess what just happened!" Linda cried.

"Miss Duncan called us into her office," Dot added, "and–"

"And told you that you had been awarded a trip to Europe," Joan said.

The other two stiffened. "How did you know?"

"I'm known as Detective Joan Bailey in these

parts," she said, "first cousin to the incomparable Sherlock Holmes. In short, I am a sleuth who knows all secrets."

"But," Linda countered, "Miss Duncan said that no one knew about it yet except the–the other two who are–" Her voice trailed off. "That means – oh, Joan! You're going too!"

"A marvelous deduction. Worthy of my incomparable first cousin–"

And then her words were lost, swallowed in the babble of voices as everybody tried to talk at once.

Felicia thought of all those things as she and Joan paused before the dingy, little hut.

"Joan," she whispered, "I–I'm scared."

Her friend half turned. "Why don't we go back to the village?"

"We–we can't," she stammered. "I promised Great-Uncle Don."

"But why?" Joan insisted. "We'll never even see them again."

Back home, the night before flying, it had seemed so simple to agree to help Great-Uncle Don's friends.

"I don't know whether I told you or not," he had said, "but there was a French couple who saved me from the Nazis during the war when my plane was shot down over French territory."

Felicia had nodded. How could she help remembering? His letters had been filled with stories of them when she was a little girl.

"When I wrote that you were going over, they asked if you would help them with an errand." Great-Uncle Don had paused then, significantly.

"What sort of an errand?"

"They didn't say," he had added. "But, Felicia, Duvall and his wife saved my life. It would mean a great deal to me if you'd go and see them."

It was the next day that Great-Uncle Don had given her directions to get from the village to the Duvall cottage.

"I talked with them for hours about the Savior," he had confided. "I might have been able to have helped Henri spiritually if it hadn't been for his wife. She's a hard-nosed old girl, Felicia, and set in her ways. Claims to be an atheist. And she acted it too." He had moved across the living room slowly and turned before the fireplace. "But in spite of that, she and Henri saved my life. I'll always be indebted to them."

Great-Uncle Don had asked her if she would talk with the old couple again about Christ.

"The years haven't been too easy with them according to what they've written," he had said. "It may be that they are softer now and that they'll listen to the gospel."

"I'll do what I can," Felicia had promised.

She had been so excited about the trip that she hadn't thought much about the visit to the Duvalls when their plane landed at LeHavre and the little group began to tour France. She had thought little about it until that very morning when they reached the village, and Joan informed her that she had promised her Great-Uncle Don that she would go and see the elderly couple. But now, as she and Joan stood before the little peasant cottage, the moisture came out on her forehead, and she was trembling inside.

"Well," Joan exclaimed in that matter-of-fact tone of hers, "are we going into the house or aren't we?"

Felicia opened the gate. "I–I suppose we've got to go."

"I know. We promised your Great-Uncle Don." She followed her friend into the yard. "That conscience of yours is going to get me killed yet."

Felicia giggled nervously.

"Now listen," she countered. "You know that you wouldn't miss this for anything."

"Just try me!" she said. "Just try me on that."

In spite of her words, however, she was half a step ahead of Felicia, and her eyes were glittering expectantly.

They had only taken a few steps up the lane toward the cottage when a man appeared out of the shadows and stood before them. A tall man with a limp.

"Oh!" Joan gasped. She froze, immobile.

Felicia clutched at the sleeve of her jacket.

"W-w-what do you want?" the Cartright girl demanded.

"Are you going to see the Duvalls?" the man

asked softly in English. There was the faintest trace of accent to his voice.

"If that's where they live, we're certainly going to see them," Joan broke in briskly, "if you'll step aside, that is."

"You are strangers here."

Felicia stepped back, almost involuntarily.

"The Duvalls took my great-uncle in and hid him from the Nazis when his fighter plane was shot down over France during the war," she explained. "He asked us to come and see them."

"We would talk with you, Mademoiselle." He took his credentials from his pocket and handed them to Felicia. Joan, who was staring over her shoulder, caught her breath sharply.

"The police! But we haven't done anything!"

Felicia's heart caught in her throat.

"Then you have nothing to be afraid of," he answered. "This way, please."

"But where are you taking us?" the Cartright girl insisted.

"To a place where we can ask you a few questions." He took the girls firmly by their arms and guided them back on the road to a spot where a small French car was secreted.

CHAPTER 2

A SUSPICIOUS OFFICER

Joan Bailey hung back reluctantly.

"Miss Duncan isn't going to like this," she informed him. "When she hears what has happened to us, she's going to be furious."

His forehead crinkled quizzically. "And who is Mademoiselle Duncan?" he asked.

Joan's eyes were aflame.

"If you don't let us go, you'll find out who Miss Duncan is. And quick!"

The Frenchman shrugged his shoulders expressively.

"You American girls. You try to frighten everyone."

Felicia got into the back seat of the pint-sized French car, and Joan followed her.

"What do you suppose he's going to do to us?" she whispered in the Cartright girl's ear.

Felicia shook her head. "He can't do much. We're

American citizens, and we haven't been breaking any French laws."

"Unless it's against the law to visit with your Great-Uncle Don's friends." She shuddered. "I hate to think of what they must be like if the authorities get suspicious of everyone who comes to visit them."

The officer drove into the little village, past the police station, to a small hotel where he stopped.

"I thought you said you were going to take us to the station," Felicia said in passable French.

"We would prefer to talk with you here."

By this time darkness enveloped the village, closing in around the small, poorly lighted homes.

"And we would prefer to go to the police station where we can get in touch with the American Consul," Felicia told him sharply.

He opened the door for them.

"It will pay Mademoiselle not to be difficult." He took their arms once more and guided them to the squat little building that served the village as a second hotel. Anyone seeing them would have thought a father was taking his daughters to dinner or that perhaps they were with an old family friend. But his grip on their arms was steel, and his voice was commanding, for all of its softness. "I have already called ahead. There will be a policewoman in the room upstairs to search you.

"To search us?" Joan cried indignantly.

"Precisely. Now if Mademoiselle will be so good

as to lower her voice and to refrain from outbursts in the lobby."

"B-b-but hauling us in and searching us like c-c-common thieves," Joan spluttered.

He paused before the door and laid a warning finger to his lips.

The girls looked around desperately as he steered them through the lobby and up dilapidated, squeaking stairs, but it was empty except for a clerk nodding at the desk.

In the hotel room, two plump, round-faced women in severe uniforms came forward and took the girls from the officer.

"If you will come in here, my dear," one of them said to Felicia, "we will conduct the examination. It will only take a moment."

"But we haven't done anything," Felicia said hotly. "We're American citizens, and we were minding our own business. You have no right to–to–"

"We don't treat your people this way when they come over to America," Joan snapped.

For answer the women took the two girls into the next room and closed the door. Two or three minutes later they returned.

"Well?" the officer asked, his face lighting expectantly.

"Nothing."

"Nothing?" his eyes grew round.

"Nothing. Absolutely nothing."

For a long minute he did not answer. He picked up the girls' passports and began to examine them.

"Your papers are all in order," he said at last.

"That's what we've been trying to tell you."

"And you have never seen the Duvalls before today?" There was a question in his voice.

"We didn't even get to see them today," Joan retorted. "Remember?"

"We are so very sorry to have embarrassed you."

"I should think you would be," she said hotly. "Are you satisfied now that we haven't stolen the Eiffel Tower? Or is it the Cathedral of Notre Dame that is missing?"

"A thousand pardons, Mademoiselle," he said, sweeping low in a bow.

Felicia and Joan stood before him. "Are we free to go?" the Cartright girl asked at last.

"*Oui,* Mademoiselle, you are free to go. And please accept our humble apologies."

Joan thrust out her hand impulsively. "I'm sorry I spouted off the way I did to you," she said. "I was angry. But I shouldn't have been. You were only doing your duty."

He took her hand gravely and pressed his lips to it. Felicia snickered.

When they were outside, Joan turned to her. "I could have clobbered you in there," she said darkly. "He was just being polite."

"I didn't say a word. Not a single word."

"You didn't have to."

They crossed the street in silence.

"Do you suppose we dare go back out to the Duvalls now?" Felicia asked.

Joan turned to face her. "Do you actually mean that you want to go back out there?" she demanded. "At night?"

"It's our only chance. Miss Duncan has our itinerary all planned. We move on tomorrow."

"But she'll skin us alive if we don't get back to the hotel at a decent hour. You know how she is back at Wellington."

"They won't be back to the village until the two o'clock train," Felicia reminded her.

"I was hoping you'd forget that the way I had," Joan told her.

"We've got to go, Joan," Felicia said again. "You know that Miss Duncan won't wait for us to see the Duvalls in the morning."

"All right." She sighed her resignation. "I guess I'm ready. It won't be any worse for me than it will for you. But I would like to see dear old Wellington just once more before I go."

"Silly!" Felicia exclaimed.

They left the village and walked down the narrow, winding road to the cottage.

"It's awfully dark, isn't it?" Felicia asked, her voice quavering uncertainly.

"I like it better that way," her companion informed

her. "If a big old dragon is going to leap out of the ditch and swallow us, I don't want to see him first."

"You're a big help on this trip."

"The only place I'd be any good is back in our hotel," Joan said. She glanced around. "I–I didn't even know that it could get so dark."

"There's a light," Felicia broke in. "That must be Duvalls'."

"Well, come on," her friend said crisply. "If we've got to see them, we'd just as well get it over with."

"I suppose you're right."

They went up to the door hesitantly and knocked.

"M-maybe there's nobody home," Joan whispered hopefully.

Felicia started to answer but stopped suddenly as they heard the muffled sound of heavy footsteps and the protesting creak of the bolt in the lock.

The door opened, and the faint yellow circle of light revealed the tattered dress and straggly gray hair of the woman who was standing there. She was spare and sharp featured, and her arthritic hands were twisted and bony. She was a pale, forlorn creature, except for her eyes. They burned with a strange, cold fire that seemed to pierce to the very depths of Felicia's heart. Almost instinctively she drew back.

"What do you want?" the old woman demanded, her voice cracking.

"Are you Mrs. Duvall?" the Cartright girl asked.

"My husband is not at home." She moved as though to close the door. "What do you want with Duvall?"

"One thing we'd like to know," Joan said crisply, "is what's going on here. First, we get hauled in by the police and questioned and searched. Now you're going to shut the door in our faces. Just what is this, anyway?"

The old woman's face darkened, and, for a fleeting instant, fear flashed across it.

"The police?" she echoed, leaning forward and lowering her voice. "It is not the police who watch our humble, little cottage."

The girls stiffened.

"Who was it that grabbed us then," Felicia demanded, "and hauled us down to the hotel?"

The old woman stared past them, first one direction and then the other, as though straining to see something in the darkness.

"The same ones who came and searched our place a fortnight ago," she told them.

"And who would that be?" Joan insisted.

"The Communists! They are everywhere!"

CHAPTER 3

"HE'S MY UNCLE!"

"**C**ommunists!"

Felicia knew that her face went ashen, and her hands began to tremble. Joan, who was standing beside her, sucked in her breath with a quick, hissing sound.

"S-s-shh!" the old woman warned, putting a finger to her lips. "When it comes to the Communists, everything has ears. They are everywhere."

"But why would they want to bother an old couple like you and your husband?" Joan asked brashly. "If you'll pardon my saying so, it doesn't look to me as though you have anything they would want, and I know that Felicia and I don't have. We don't ever have any money."

Madame Duvall acted as though she had not heard Joan. "And why do you come to bother an old

17

woman and her husband?" she insisted. "We have done nothing to you."

Felicia felt cold chills crawl up her spine.

"Do you remember Don Morgan?" she asked. "The American?"

The old lady's forehead wrinkled. "And who is he?"

"He's my great-uncle," she explained. "He asked us to come and see you." Felicia smiled briefly, trying hard to be friends, but Madame Duvall's bleak gaze frosted the smile as soon as it touched her lips.

"You will have to talk with Henri," she said coldly, stepping back and motioning them inside.

The two girls followed her, hesitantly, into the small, dimly lit room. She did not ask them to be seated.

After a moment or two a wizened, sharp-nosed little Frenchman came hobbling out of a side door that must have come from a bedroom. He, too, was gray and twisted with age.

"Good evening," Felicia said pleasantly. But the man did not return her greeting. Instead, his eyes found hers, and for a moment, held them in battle.

"She says that she is a niece of the American, Donald Morgan," Madame Duvall informed him. "You remember the American."

The old man's eyes narrowed to thin, watery slits.

"Does she tell the truth, Mama?"

The old woman shrugged her shoulders. "Why would two girls come from the American?" she asked. "And in the dark of night?"

"This one looks like him," her husband countered slowly. "He has the same color. The same look about the eyes. The same straw-colored hair."

She nodded cryptically. "But how can we be sure?" There was suspicion in her voice.

"What did your great-uncle tell you about us?" M'sieu Duvall asked. "Why did he stay with us? What happened while he was here?"

Hurriedly Felicia told him all that her Great-Uncle Don had told her. "And," she concluded, "there was an Englishman hiding with you at the same time. A short, fat man."

"Was there anyone else?"

"A flier from–," she thought momentarily, "from Poland, I believe."

The old man's eyes gleamed, but his expression did not change.

"His name?" he asked. "Do you remember his name?"

"I think so." She drew her lips down narrowly. "I believe it was – Wolejaska or something like that."

Both Madame and M'sieu Duvall leaned forward expectantly.

"And what did your uncle do while he was here?"

"What do you mean?"

"What did he talk about?"

Felicia moistened her lips with the tip of her tongue. "He talked with you about Jesus Christ," she said. "He read to you from his New Testament about how a man must be born again. How he must confess his sin and put his trust in the Lord Jesus Christ if he is to be saved. He told you how much Christ meant to him."

The elderly couple stared at one another for a long moment, beaming.

"They tell the truth, Mama!" Henri Duvall exclaimed. "They tell the truth about the American sending them to see us."

Madame Duvall got to her feet, silently, and moved to the window.

"Papa!" she cried, her thin voice trembling. "Someone is coming along the road!"

Fright clouded her husband's eyes and twisted his thin face. "Quick! In here!" He almost pushed Felicia and Joan toward the bedroom.

"What's the matter?" Joan asked. She was trying to stare past M'sieu Duvall to see out the window.

"It is no matter, Henri," Madame Duvall said, breathing her relief. "It is just Pierre coming home from the village. He went in this afternoon to sell a cow."

The old man sighed wearily.

"All our lives it seems that we have been hiding from this one and that. First it was the Nazis and now the Communists." He shook his head miserably. "We are not so fortunate as you in America."

Madame Duvall came back to where the American girls were standing, still breathing heavily. For the first time she motioned for them to sit down. She sat down across from them in a spindling, straight-backed chair.

"We know now that we can trust you," she said, lowering her voice confidentially. "Such a fine Christian as Don Morgan would only send Christians to see us."

Felicia smiled. "We do know the Lord as our Savior," she said.

"This man you spoke of a moment ago," the old woman continued. "His name is Wolejeski rather than Wolejaska."

"I couldn't have come that close," Joan said, "and I heard Felicia's Great-Uncle Don mention it too."

Madame Duvall nodded. "The name is Wolejeski, but that is of small matter. The important thing is that you are in a position to save his life!"

The girls stared at her incredulously. "But how?" Felicia demanded. "What could we possibly do that would save him?"

"A simple thing," M'sieu Duvall put in. "A very simple thing. But so important."

"*Oui,*" his wife added. "He is detained at this very moment and in terrible danger for his friendliness toward America and American ideals. We want you to deliver something to–"

"Now wait a minute," Joan broke in. "We aren't going into Communist territory for anybody."

"*Non,*" the old man said, shaking his head. "*Non,* it is not there that we ask you to go."

Madame Duvall took a small box from a pocket deep in the folds of her bulky dress and held it momentarily in her bony fingers. "If you can get this to Antwerp, where it can be smuggled to him in Poland, he can use it to buy the forged papers that he needs to get over to the West and your beloved United States."

Felicia's head swirled and perspiration pearled her forehead.

"You will help, won't you?"

"You see," Henri explained, "when Wolejeski left us with the French underground after his plane was shot down during the war, he was afraid that he would be caught by the Nazis. And so he entrusted this box with us. Now he had a letter smuggled out of Poland and brought to us. He needs it desperately. It will be life and freedom for him."

Neither of the girls could speak.

"Everything has been arranged," Madame Duvall whispered. "If only you will help." She opened the box and held it before them. They both gasped!

"An uncut diamond!" Henri Duvall exclaimed. *"And worth enough to buy Wolejeski's way to freedom!"*

CHAPTER 4

A STRANGE REQUEST

For a long minute Felicia and Joan stared at the box in the aged woman's hand. The tiny Chinese jewel case was the thing that first attracted their attention. The lacquered box was a work of art, made of countless coats of paint and intricately carved by hand.

"Oh!" Joan exclaimed. "How beautiful!"

"It is the diamond that is valuable," Henri Duvall snapped curtly.

The rough uncut stone didn't appear to be valuable. It was about the size of a pigeon egg, or a little larger, but was as dull and unpromising as a chunk of glass.

"Is that really a diamond?" Joan asked brashly. "It certainly doesn't look like much."

"That is because the tools of Antwerp haven't released its beauty," Madame Duvall said. "Let a skilled diamond cutter go to work on it and you will see how magnificent it is. It is a diamond, all right."

"But it is so large," Felicia murmured, taking the stone gently in her fingers. "It must be worth a lot."

Old Henri Duvall leaned forward. "That is right, Mademoiselle. It is worth a lot. At this moment, it is worth a very brave man's life."

Felicia glanced at her friend quizzically.

"I know you'll agree to it," Joan told her, "so I'd just as well forget about arguing and agree too."

"And what is it that you want us to do?" Felicia asked. She spoke reluctantly. "If we should agree to help you and this Wolejeski."

"Wolejeski has a cousin in Antwerp," the old woman said, her voice breaking with emotion. "All we ask of you is that you will take this stone to him. He will see that it gets to its destination."

"If that's all you want done," Joan asked, "why didn't you mail it?"

Duvall's face clouded. "You do not understand. There are men who would *kill* to get possession of this diamond."

"K-k-kill?" Joan echoed.

He nodded grimly. "That is why it is so important that you carry it. No one will suspect you."

"If it is so urgent that Wolejeski's cousin get possession of this stone so quickly," Felicia asked, turning the matter thoughtfully in her mind, "why did you wait for us to come and deliver it to Antwerp?"

The elderly couple glanced at one another.

"It is a matter of trust," Madame Duvall broke in. "Henri and I are old. No longer could we make such a trip."

Henri nodded vigorously. "It has been three years now since we have made a trip even so far away as Paris. We could never stand to travel all the way to Antwerp. But you we can trust."

"How do you know that you can trust us?" Joan asked.

"You have come in answer to your Great-Uncle Don's request," M'sieu Duvall answered, "and you are Christians. That is enough for me."

Felicia was silent for a moment.

"If this matter of being a Christian means so much to you," she said, "if you have so much confidence in Christians, even two Christians you have never met before, you must think much of the power of the gospel of Christ."

A strange look came into the old couples' eyes.

"We do," Henri stammered.

Felicia stepped forward earnestly. "Have you ever considered the claims of the Savior for yourself?" she asked. "Have you ever thought that you two are sinners and need a Savior?"

The old man's face grew cold.

"Some other time. When you have completed our mission." He spoke with finality. "That is, if you will do as we ask you to do."

The Cartright girl nodded her agreement.

"If you'll give us the address of this Wolejeski's cousin in Antwerp," she said, taking a notebook from her purse, "we'll take the package to him. I think Miss Duncan is planning on taking us to Belgium next."

Madame Duvall smiled.

"You are naive, Mademoiselle." She lowered her voice significantly. "We must move very carefully to protect you and the others. You would not be safe for a moment if we were to go about delivering the diamond so openly. Your instructions will be waiting for you when you arrive at your hotel in Antwerp."

"But why not let us have them now?" Joan asked. "I can't see what possible difference it would make for us to know how we are to make contact in Antwerp."

Madame Duvall's eyes flashed. "We will do the thinking," she snapped. "You are to follow instructions."

"When you get our instructions in Antwerp," her husband continued, "take them to your room before opening them. Read them carefully and burn them."

Felicia glanced at her watch. "If you'll give us the box now," she said, "we'll have to be going. Miss Duncan and the others will be back at the hotel before long."

"But you are not to leave the house now! It isn't safe!"

"We have to go. Miss Duncan is expecting us."

"But those men who stopped you," Madame Duvall

added. "They may still be lurking outside. We can't let you take the box as long as there is danger that they are there."

"Then we'll have to go without it," Joan said quickly. I've tangled with Miss Duncan before."

"One moment." The old woman turned toward the bedroom door. "I will wrap the box."

Joan turned, and when the old man wasn't looking, she stooped and picked up a small piece of cardboard on the floor.

Felicia saw it and questioned her with her eyes, but Joan shook her head almost imperceptibly.

"Do you have much company?" she asked when Madame Duvall returned with the box wrapped in heavy brown paper and securely tied.

"*Non,*" she said, shaking her head. "No one ever comes to see old folks like us. And with the Communists so busy, it is as well. There's no knowing whom you can trust these days."

She handed the package to Felicia. "Guard it well. If you lose it, you will be signing the death warrant of an innocent man."

Felicia shuddered.

"W-we'll do our best."

She put the box in her backpack and started for the door, but Joan made no move to leave.

"Do you get out of the village often?" she asked.

Henri's face crinkled questioningly.

"What do you mean?" There was suspicion in his voice.

"Do you get to Paris very often?" she went on.

"To Paris?" he echoed, shrugging his shoulders expressively. "How long has it been since we have been to Paris, Mama?"

"A long time," she said. "A very long time. It's been years, I think."

"Oui" her husband agreed quickly. "Maybe ten years or more."

"And you have had no company for a month?" she persisted.

Madame Duvall's face darkened.

"It has been six months since we had company," Henri said, "until you came today."

"You act as though you do not believe us," his wife exclaimed. "We are honest people. We are not used to having people doubt our words."

Joan would have said more, but Felicia took her by the arm. "We must go," she said. "Miss Duncan and the girls will be back any time."

"Guard the box well," Madame Duvall whispered, "and follow the instructions carefully."

Then they were out in the cold, forbidding darkness. For an instant they stood before the tiny peasant cottage, staring around them.

"C-c-come on," Felicia said, her voice breaking. "I'll feel better when we get to the hotel."

"So will I." They walked rapidly out to the gate and up the road to the village.

"What do you make of it?" the Cartright girl asked after a moment or two.

"I don't like it," Joan retorted. "None of it."

"The Duvalls are strange," Felicia acknowledged.

"They're more than that," Joan went on firmly. "They lied to us."

"What makes you say that?" Felicia shifted the backpack uneasily from one hand to the other.

"They said they haven't been to Paris for years," Joan answered, "and that it's been six months since they had company."

"What does that have to do with it?" Felicia asked.

"I found a train ticket stub to Paris on the floor in there," she said with a toss of her head. "And according to the date, it's less than two weeks old."

The Cartright girl stopped suddenly. "What do you suppose that means?" she asked.

"I don't know," Joan said slowly. "But it makes me wonder what sort of mess we're actually in."

"There must be some logical explanation for it," Felicia said. "After all, it makes no difference to us whether they've been to Paris recently or not."

"But Felicia," Joan said, "if they would lie to us about one thing, they might be lying to us about something else."

"What can we do about it?" her friend asked.

"We've already taken the diamond and have agreed to deliver it."

Joan threw her hands into the air. "I knew it," she wailed. "When I agreed to go with you to see the Duvalls, I knew that trouble was coming. Every time I say I'm not going to get mixed up in your schemes, but somehow you hook me into it."

"If we don't hurry and get back before Miss Duncan does, we'll both be mixed up in something we won't care for."

"You can say that again."

Fortunately, when they got back to the hotel, Miss Duncan and her companions had not yet returned. They did not see her until the following morning at breakfast.

"Well," the chaperone began primly, "did you get your business transacted, Felicia?"

The Cartright girl felt her cheeks tinge with color. "We–we got to see the Duvalls," she acknowledged.

"You missed a most enjoyable concert," Miss Duncan said, "and before that, a thrilling trip to the museum. We wished you had been with us, didn't we, girls?"

Linda and Dot nodded dutifully.

"There was a time or two when we wished that we were with you too," Joan told them.

The two girls leaned forward excitedly. "When was that?" one of them demanded. "What happened?"

"The Duvalls were strange people," Felicia said uneasily. "They sort of gave us the creeps."

"I was against it," Miss Duncan said. "I was against your leaving us from the start. I should have gone out to their home with you."

"We got back safely enough," Joan said. "And that's the main thing."

"I should never have forgiven myself if anything had happened to you." Miss Duncan laughed nervously. "But I don't know why I should think anything would happen to you. France is a civilized country."

The waiter who had come up behind them just then nodded gravely.

"*Oui,* Mademoiselle," he said. "France is a civilized country."

The train was to leave about noon, and Miss Duncan excused herself to go and finish packing.

"But mind you," she said, "be back here at the hotel at 11:00."

"Why don't you go shopping with Linda and Dot?" Joan suggested to Felicia. "I've got an errand to run."

"Can't we all go together?" Dot asked.

Joan shook her head.

"Why don't you let us in on things too?" Linda said, pleading. "You have all the fun."

"My dear little soulmate from Wellington," Joan said, "I am sorry to inform you that my errand is not exactly going to be fun."

With that, she left before they had a chance to

protest further. She went into one small shop, out by a side door, and crossed to the police station.

The officer at the desk looked up at her respectfully.

"You are looking for someone, Mademoiselle?" he asked.

She hesitated, and for a brief instant fought down the desire to flee.

"I am looking for a tall man," she said at last. "A man with a limp."

The French officer shook his head.

"We have only poor old Pierre in our jail," he said. "And he is as fat as the lard bucket. He waddles, but he does not limp. I am sorry, Mademoiselle."

"No," she insisted. "I want to talk with one of the police officers. A tall man who limps."

The man's face grew perplexed.

"We have no officer like that, Mademoiselle. Ours is only a little village. There is–"

"I–I see," she said, turning toward the door. "I must have made a mistake."

CHAPTER 5

THE MESSAGE AT ANTWERP

Miss Duncan and the girls were waiting in the lobby of the hotel when Joan came hurrying up to join them.

"Well," the woman said, "it is now 11:03, Joan. I suppose you tried to get back on time."

"I had an errand to run, Miss Duncan," she explained.

Miss Duncan would have said more, but the hotel clerk came up to her, bowing.

"Mademoiselle," he said courteously, "you asked me to inform you when it was time to leave for the train."

"Thank you, my good man." She dropped a small coin into his hand.

He glanced at it and frowned his disapproval.

"Come, girls," Miss Duncan said, clapping her

hands briskly. "We must hurry to the station. We haven't yet bought our tickets."

There were no cabs in the village, and they had to walk, carrying their baggage.

Joan signaled Felicia with a toss of her head, and they hung back a few paces so the others couldn't hear. "And so," she concluded, whispering hurriedly, "we know that the police don't even have a tall man who limps on the force."

"I don't understand this at all."

"What is it that you don't understand?" Dot broke in. Neither Felicia nor Joan had noticed that she had dropped back too and was listening. "What's going on here anyway?"

"Come, girls. We must hurry. Time and railroad trains wait for no one."

They got to the station, Miss Duncan bought the tickets, and they all sat down to wait.

"Now listen, you two," Dot said feverishly. "We know that something is going on, and we want in on it. What gives?"

"Oh, look!" Joan said quickly, winking at Felicia, and pointing to a young French couple. "They must be newly married. See how she hangs on his arm."

"Isn't that lovely?" the Cartright girl said, taking her cue from Joan. "I hope we get to sit close to them on the train. They're so cute."

Miss Duncan was back by that time. Joan and Felicia sighed thankfully as she began to give them a running account of the battles that had been fought in that region.

Soon the train came in. There were others who got on too. The bride and groom were first, giggling nervously, an old man with a long stick of bread under his arm, and two or three soldiers on leave from Algiers.

Miss Duncan, sitting across from Felicia, began to nod. Dot and Linda noted it, and their eyes lit up expectantly. In a few minutes she would be asleep. And then the questions would come, furiously. Felicia glanced over at Joan.

The Bailey girl leaned back and closed her eyes. Felicia looked out the window at the passing landscape for a time, then opened her purse and got out her small Bible. In the bustle of the morning, she had forgotten her devotions.

"Do you always make such a show of Bible reading, Felicia?" Linda asked. She meant to sound cheerful and bantering, but there was a bite to her words.

"I usually read the Bible every day," Felicia told her. "At least I try to."

Linda snorted.

"I don't see what you can get out of that," she said. "It's dry as dust to me."

"That's because you don't read it enough," Felicia explained. "The Bible is the Word of God, Linda. It presents to us the claims of the Lord Jesus Christ as Savior."

Linda smiled at her.

"Surely you're not naive enough to believe that," she countered. "Haven't you studied science?"

"I haven't studied a thing that has shaken my faith in either the Bible or in Jesus Christ," the Cartright girl told her. "I confessed my sin and put my trust in Him to save me. And, Linda, the Lord has meant more to me with every new day."

Joan opened her eyes. "I used to say the same things you've said just now, Linda, but that was before I examined the claims of Christ and came to see that He was the answer to the problems in my life. And I'm happier than I've ever been before."

Linda Hodges turned from her companions to stare out the window at the passing scene. Her eyes grew pensive, and when she finally looked back at Felicia, there was a softness there. A softness and a nameless longing that had never been in her face before. Dot Craig listened quietly but did not speak.

Felicia put away her Bible and closed her eyes to pray. So very much had happened the past few hours.

It was almost evening when they reached the Belgian border and started through customs. Felicia shifted uneasily. The package was in the bottom of her backpack. She had to declare it! And if she did, it would be taken away!

Before she reached the desk, an official spotted her in the line.

"You, Mademoiselle," he said curtly. "Will you please come into my office?"

"M-me?" she stammered.

"*Oui.* I must talk with you."

Miss Duncan pushed forward. "I am responsible for these girls," she announced. "If you are going to take Felicia anywhere, I demand that I be permitted to go along."

"But *non,* Mademoiselle," he told her patiently. "I would talk with her for a moment or two. Alone."

"You aren't going to take her away from here!" It was half statement, half question.

"For one moment," he informed her. And then, before Miss Duncan had an opportunity to follow, he whisked Felicia through a door and closed it peremptorily.

"Now, Mademoiselle," he said, lowering his voice, "do you have a small black box for Antwerp?"

Perspiration moistened Felicia's forehead, and she grasped her purse tightly.

"Yes," she said in a small voice.

"Good. I have been expecting you."

Felicia stared at him quizzically.

"Come, Mademoiselle," he said, his voice suddenly brisk and businesslike. "Your passport, please."

At that moment Miss Duncan and a police officer came bursting into the office.

"There he is!" she announced triumphantly, stabbing at the official with her umbrella. "He snatched one of the girls in my care and dragged her in here against her will."

"It was all a mistake," the customs official said blandly, with the faintest of smiles in Felicia's direction. "We must constantly be on the alert for smugglers."

Miss Duncan's face was stern.

"Do I look like a smuggler?" she demanded. "Does the American government make a practice of issuing passports to smugglers?"

"Miss Cartright's papers are in order." He touched his cap and bowed slightly. "A thousand pardons."

"I should think so." The teacher grasped Felicia by the arm and marched her outside. "If anything like this happens again," she continued, her eyes snapping, "and I am not present, insist on calling the American Consul."

"Miss Duncan," Felicia began, "I think I should tell you that I–

The chaperone shook her head. "Not a word, Felicia. Not another word. We are on a holiday. We aren't going to permit an oafish official to blight it." She squeezed Felicia's arm understandingly and surprised her with a slow, deliberate wink.

They went on into Antwerp without incident, and Miss Duncan guided them to the hotel where they had reservations.

"The evening is free," she said as they entered the lobby. "We'll discuss what we are going to do at dinner."

The clerk had mail for them. Miss Duncan took charge of it and parceled it out briskly.

"Here is a letter for you, Felicia," she said. "I didn't know you had friends in France."

The Cartright girl felt the breath squeeze out of her. Her fingers were shaking as she took it.

"Who's it from?" Dot asked, trying to peer over her shoulder. "A boyfriend?"

"Aren't you going to open it?" Linda insisted.

Felicia knew that her face must be scarlet, but she put the letter into her purse.

Not until she and Joan were in their room did she open the letter.

"Is it from the Duvalls?" Joan Bailey whispered, checking to make sure that the door was locked.

Felicia moved closer to the naked light bulb that was suspended from the ceiling.

"The handwriting is that of someone much younger," she said.

"But what does it say?"

By this time, she had opened the envelope and removed a single sheet of paper.

"We have notified the minister of a small, evangelical church that you and your party are Christians," she read. "He will call, asking you to attend church tonight. When the meeting is over, leave the building immediately. At the bottom of the steps turn left. In English, say to the man who is standing there, 'A nice service, wasn't it?' He will reply in French, 'It would have been nicer in English.' That will indicate to you that he is the proper man. Give the box to him."

"That's strange," Joan said thoughtfully. "Imagine using a church for a contact."

Felicia shivered involuntarily. "I'll be mighty glad to be through with this," she observed. "I almost wish we hadn't agreed to it."

Before Joan could answer there was a crisp knock on the door.

"Good news, girls!" Miss Duncan sang out. "Good news!"

The Bailey girl strode to the door and opened it.

"I'm glad to see that you show caution in keeping your room locked," she said, nodding to Joan. "Caution is an admirable trait. A most admirable trait."

Joan smiled warmly.

Miss Duncan had them call Linda and Dot into their room.

"Now," she said when they were all together, "we don't have to decide what to do this evening. Someone informed the pastor of a small church here in Antwerp that we were in town," she said excitedly, "and he called to give us a special invitation to attend their service tonight."

"That sounds interesting," Joan replied, trying hard to sound surprised.

Dot Craig snorted her disgust.

"Our first night in Antwerp," she exclaimed, "and we've got to spend it in church!"

"It will be an excellent place for you to practice your French," the chaperone informed her.

"But I don't want to practice my French."

Miss Duncan's manner stiffened. "From the looks of your grade in the subject last semester," she said, "you should want to practice your French, Dorothy. The matter is closed." She spoke with finality. "I have already told the minister that we will be happy to attend."

Linda and Dot both scowled.

Miss Duncan saw the look on their faces but chose to ignore it.

"Get dressed quickly, girls. It is not ladylike to rush dinner, and we must hurry if we are to be in church on time."

As soon as the others went to their rooms, Felicia got into her coat and put the small package into a deep pocket.

"Do you know the instructions we're to follow?" Joan asked. "We've got to destroy that letter. If Miss Duncan found it, we'd have some embarrassing explanations to make."

Felicia took the letter, tore it to bits, and secreted it under the paper lining in a dresser drawer.

"Now," her companion said, relieved, "she'll never find it."

"In a couple of hours, we'll be rid of the package too," the Cartright girl answered, "and I can breathe easily again."

She turned out the light, and they went down to the lobby to wait for Miss Duncan.

As they came down the stairs, a man in a chair by the window glanced up casually.

Joan started and grasped Felicia's arm.

"What's the matter?" she asked almost irritably.

"Don't look now, but does that man over there seem familiar to you?"

Felicia crossed the floor slowly and turned with studied carelessness. Her body stiffened, and briefly, an almost uncontrollable urge to cry out seized her.

The man had been in the depot in the village where the Duvalls lived. Lounging carelessly then, too, but always watching. Watching!

Miss Duncan, Linda, and Dot came down then, and they went out to eat. The teacher chattered incessantly but kept close account of the time.

"Girls," she said, pushing back from the table at 7:00, "we have thirty minutes to walk over to the church."

"I hope we get lost," Linda muttered under her breath.

"Have no fear of that," Miss Duncan said without breaking stride. "I have studied the map carefully. We should be able to make our way to the church without complication and see a bit of the charm of Antwerp after dark as well."

They found the church easily enough, and Miss Duncan guided them into a pew near the back.

Felicia glanced around the small congregation. The faces were so solemn, so sincere. Which one would approach her after the service?

CHAPTER 6

THE CONTACT INTERRUPTED

The minister noted the five Americans as they came in and nodded a greeting from the platform. The congregation finished singing, and the pastor launched into his message.

Felicia thought she could understand French quite well, but he spoke so rapidly that she had difficulty in following him. Linda, who was sitting next to her, fidgeted uneasily. At first the Cartright girl thought she wasn't listening, but her face was serious, and a trapped, haunted look reflected in her eyes.

There was a young American couple sitting toward the front of the church. Felicia spotted them as her gaze wandered over the congregation. The boy was tall with a typical American haircut, and she was wearing clothes and a coat that could only have come from the States.

It would be nice to meet them. And then she

remembered! There was someone waiting for her outside.

When the benediction was over, Felicia turned and hurried back to the door. Joan was scrambling to join her. She wanted desperately to wait for her friend, but she dared not. Even now her contact should be outside, anxious to get the diamond and get away.

Felicia stepped out into the chilly, foggy night and glanced around uncertainly. If there was anyone there, she couldn't see him. Then the darkness seemed to stir, and a great, shadowy hulk of a man emerged from it.

Felicia shuddered as the clammy fingers of fear enveloped her. She knew the man was there, but that was all. Wrapped in a heavy, dark coat, he was only a large, unidentifiable shape.

The Cartright girl's heart quickened. Perspiration beaded her forehead. She tried to speak, but her voice had a strange, croaking sound.

"Good evening," she managed in English, struggling hard to keep from revealing the fear that had seized her. "A nice service, wasn't it?"

The stranger took half a step forward, eagerly, as though he had been waiting long and was eager to get the business over and be gone. He started to speak but stopped abruptly.

"Oh, there you are!" a voice behind Felicia exclaimed in broken English. "I was afraid that I had missed you. We're so glad to have you come and worship with us. We always welcome Americans."

She turned miserably. There stood the pastor, holding out his hand.

Felicia stood there helplessly. Her contact had paused momentarily as the minister came rushing out. Now he turned and melted silently into the darkness.

"It was so good of your friend to call and tell me that you were going to be in the city," the pastor said warmly.

"Friend?" Miss Duncan echoed. In the excitement, Felicia had not heard her join them. "We have no friends in Antwerp."

"No matter," the pastor replied genially. "I'm grateful for whoever called me. We have some other Americans who worship with us. I'd like to have you meet them."

Almost mechanically, Felicia permitted herself to be guided back into the church foyer. Linda and Dorothy had already been introduced to the Americans and were talking with considerable animation.

"This is Jean Anderson," the pastor said. "And this is Bill Hogan."

"Miss Anderson is a registered nurse," Miss Duncan explained, "who is going out as a missionary to the Democratic Republic of Congo."

"If I ever master French," the girl said, laughing.

"And Mr. Hogan is an exchange student," the teacher continued.

"From Texas," he added, as though that were the most important piece of information. His eyes twinkled merrily, and a smile played hide-and-seek with the corners of his mouth.

"From Texas," Miss Duncan repeated, wrinkling her nose.

The group visited for a few minutes in the back of the church, talking eagerly about home. Jean Anderson and the Texan had been overseas for some time and were very lonely.

"What I can't understand," Dot said frankly, her youthful face a question mark, "is how could you even think of throwing your life away on a bunch of uneducated pagans, Jean? Why are you going to Africa when you are needed so badly as a nurse at home?"

The missionary smiled.

"It isn't so hard to explain," she said. "It's because of the love of Christ. He died on the cross for the Africans the same as He did for me. And He called me to Africa. That's where He wants me to serve."

Dot shrugged. "You sound just like Felicia and Joan," she said. "But I still don't get it. It doesn't make sense to me."

There was a short, embarrassed silence.

"I've got an idea," Bill Hogan broke in. "I know the most charming, little restaurant. Why don't we go over and have something to eat? I'm so hungry to hear good old American speech that I can hardly stand it. Besides, I'd like to have a few minutes to tell you about the wonders of Texas." He glanced significantly at Miss Duncan. "I have a sneaking suspicion that Texas is not completely appreciated by you all."

It was then that Miss Duncan noticed how pale Felicia had become. Ignoring the wave of laughter that greeted his remark, she turned to the Cartright girl.

"My dear!" she exclaimed. "Your face is so pale. Do you feel all right?"

Felicia brushed her forehead with a shaking hand. "I–I think so," she said hesitantly.

"You don't look all right to me," the teacher said crisply. She turned to Hogan. "I am very sorry, young man. I am sure I would have found your exaggerations most amusing, but I must see that Felicia gets back to the hotel."

"I don't like to have you do that," Felicia protested. "I'll be all right."

"You do not feel like going out to a noisy cafe and listening to an equally noisy young man," Miss Duncan said. "No, we will all go back to the hotel."

Dorothy and Linda were crestfallen.

"I'll go back with Felicia, Miss Duncan," Joan broke in. "I'm awfully tired this evening anyway."

The teacher was reluctant. "Are you sure that you'll be all right?" she asked.

"Positive," Felicia assured her.

"And that you can find your way back to the hotel?"

"We'll be all right," Joan said. "And it's only a few blocks to the hotel. We'll be there and in bed before you are served."

"My only regret," Bill Hogan said, bowing deeply, "is that you girls are going to miss my brief remarks about Texas."

"Brief?" Jean said, laughing merrily. "Your remarks on Texas are brief, all right. Like a Senate filibuster."

"Now be careful," Miss Duncan warned, "and don't stop to talk with strangers."

The darkness was as thick and murky as anything the girls had ever seen before. It was a heavy, silent darkness, overlaid with a fog that shut out everything the night could not cover. It hid the streetlights from one block to the next and almost hid the lights in the buildings along the walk.

"Did you give it to him?" Joan asked when they had walked a block.

"The minister came out about ten seconds too soon."

Joan sighed. "I did the best I could to stop him, but he pushed past me and went out to where you were standing."

Felicia reached down and touched the little lacquered box in her coat pocket. It seemed now that it bulged even more conspicuously.

"What are we going to do now?"

Joan shrugged. "That's the big question."

"I wish we'd never gotten into this mess," Felicia said.

"But we are in it. Up to our little pink ears."

They had walked several blocks down the deserted street toward the hotel when Joan heard the sound of footsteps following stealthily behind them. Her breath caught sharply, and she clung to Felicia's sleeve.

"Do–do you hear anything?"

The Cartright girl stopped to listen. The footsteps stopped. "I don't hear anything."

"I don't either now," Joan answered. "But I surely did a moment ago. Footsteps."

Felicia's throat constricted. "Maybe it's our contact."

They began to walk again. She could hear the footsteps now, muffled and guarded. The two girls quickened their pace. The steps behind did the same.

"Felicia," Joan whispered, "we're three blocks from the hotel!"

"Come on!"

Bursting into a run, they dashed up the street and across the intersection. They didn't stop until they flung themselves, panting, into the lobby of the hotel.

CHAPTER 7

A THOROUGH SEARCH

The following morning was as dreary and uncomfortable as the day before. A fine spray sifted down among the ancient, weathered buildings, to be whipped by a bitter wind against the windows and the faces of people on the street. Clouds, ominously gray and forbidding, hugged the roof tops, reluctant to rain, but threatening.

Felicia awakened slowly. She rubbed the sleep from her eyes with dainty fingers and raised on one elbow to look out.

"Oh, Joan!" she exclaimed in dismay. "It's cloudy again."

"Is that news?" her roommate mumbled sleepily.

"And it's 7:30." Felicia swung her feet over the side of the bed. "Miss Duncan will be here any minute to take us down to breakfast."

"Don't you remember?" Joan asked. "This is our

shopping day in Belgium. We are free to go anywhere we wish and buy anything we can afford, as long as we don't go farther than eight blocks from the hotel."

"We're supposed to be back for a trip to the museum at 1:30," Felicia informed her. "If you don't hurry you won't even be out of bed in time for that."

"Who cares?" Joan muttered into her pillow. "All I want to do is–"

Felicia threw the covers off her.

"Felicia!" Joan cried. "It's cold! Give me those covers!"

"I'm going after some cold water," she warned, laughing. "If you're not out of bed by the time I get back–"

"Don't do that," the Bailey girl protested. "I'm getting up. I'm getting up."

They dressed and went out for breakfast together.

"See," Joan said, "there's still a light in Miss Duncan's room. That proves you dragged me out in the middle of the night."

"She's probably already had her breakfast and finished her shopping," Felicia countered, "and is waiting to take us to the museum."

"The trouble with you," Joan grumbled good-naturedly, "is that you haven't got any feelings at all."

The hotel lobby was almost empty when they went through on the way to the street. But the city had long since come to life. The cobbled streets whirred noisily with cabs and buses and were cluttered with the ever-present bicycles that were somehow every-where. The sidewalks were filled with people, silent and hurrying.

Joan stopped momentarily.

"B-r-r-r."

Felicia looked at her. "It's not that cold."

"It isn't the cold. It's this fog. It gives me the creeps."

The Cartright girl buttoned the top button of her coat. The mist and fog did give the old buildings and the streets a strange, almost furtive, appearance. There seemed to be eyes everywhere. Watching.

"Have you got the box?" Joan almost whispered.

Felicia felt the telltale bulge in her coat pocket and nodded. "I wish I knew how to get rid of it."

They walked several blocks to a little off-street cafe for breakfast.

"Do you suppose Miss Duncan knows what we're doing?" Felicia asked after a while.

"I don't see how she could," Joan replied. "We don't even know ourselves."

"I feel uneasy about not telling her."

"We haven't been lying to her," her companion said, "and we haven't deceived her by telling half-truths or anything like that. All we've done is keep our word to the Duvalls."

"I suppose you're right," Felicia said uncertainly. "I don't know how we came to get into this in the first place."

"It was to save this Wolejeski's life, remember?"

Felicia's face grew pale. "Do you suppose the fact that we missed contact last night could have ruined things?" she almost whispered.

They finished breakfast and began to look in on the shops in the neighborhood. Almost before they realized it, noon came and went.

"Felicia," Joan exclaimed, looking at her watch, "we've got to run. Miss Duncan will be anxious if we're late."

As soon as they finished their shopping, they hurried back to the hotel.

"Have you got the key?" the Cartright girl asked, fumbling in her purse.

Joan unlocked the door and threw it open.

"Felicia!" she cried.

"Joan!"

Their eyes widened and their lips drained of color.

"S-s-someone broke in here," Felicia said, stammering.

Her companion moved forward mechanically and stared around the little room. It was a shambles! Drawers had been jerked from the dresser and hurled carelessly to the floor. Their clothes had been snatched from the hangers and thrown in a heap in the middle of the threadbare rug. Pillows and mattresses had been up ended from the beds. Even the cushion in the big, overstuffed chair had been pulled out.

"That," Joan said at last, "is the understatement of the year."

"What do you suppose they were after?" Felicia asked, her voice still trembling.

"There's only one thing they could be after." Joan moved back to the door and closed it.

"The diamond?" As though she had only thought of it at that very moment. "But who would know that we have it?"

"The man who tried to make contact with us for one," Joan answered, "and the Duvalls for another."

"But they wouldn't be after it," Felicia protested. "They're the ones who gave it to us."

"I'm not so sure about anything anymore," Joan answered. "There's something strange about this whole business."

The Cartright girl walked slowly around the room. Her breath quickened. The moisture came out on the palms of her hands, and she wiped them nervously on her trim wool coat. The diamond in its beautiful, lacquered box was still in her pocket. She took it out and studied it.

"I almost wish that they had gotten it," she said, turning it in her fingers. "At least our troubles would be over then."

"We most certainly don't wish that they had gotten it," Joan countered, her voice firm and crisp. "We were supposed to get this diamond to Mr. Wolejeski's cousin. We're not going to let some common thief stop us."

Felicia slipped out of her coat and stooped quickly to pick up a pile of clothes.

"We've got to get this room straightened, Joan," she said. "If Miss Duncan comes in and finds it like this, we'll have to tell her everything."

They worked rapidly, picking up their things and making the beds again. In a short time, all was in place.

"There," Joan exclaimed, "we're ready for another visitor."

"It will probably be Miss Duncan," Felicia said, noting the time. "At least I *hope* she's the only visitor we have."

Joan put on her coat. "Let's wait for the others in the lobby," she said. "I'd like to see if that stranger is still there. The one we saw watching us last night."

Felicia shivered.

Nevertheless, she followed Joan out into the hall and tried the door after her roommate locked it.

"Mademoiselle," the clerk said blandly to Felicia as she approached, "you had a visitor while you were out."

"So we just noticed," she retorted. She spoke softly, but her voice betrayed her feelings.

"He was not in your room," the clerk said curtly, "if that is what you are inferring. We do not permit others in our guests' rooms." He reached behind him and pulled a white envelope from a pigeonhole. "He left this with me for you."

56

Felicia took the envelope and glanced at it.

"That handwriting!" Joan whispered over her shoulder. "It's the same, isn't it?"

The Cartright girl nodded almost imperceptibly. The handwriting on the envelope was identical to that on the instructions they got the day before.

They went over to a sofa in a corner and sat down.

"What does it say?" Joan whispered.

Felicia glanced around the lobby with feigned carelessness. "Do you suppose we dare look at it here?"

"We're all alone. But hurry. Miss Duncan and the others will be down any minute."

Felicia's fingers trembled slightly as she ripped the envelope and read the message.

"The service at church is going to be excellent tonight."

"We're to go back there!" Joan exclaimed.

"We might have known it." Felicia read the message again and crumpled it in her hand.

"Don't throw it away," her companion warned.

At that moment Miss Duncan, Linda, and Dot came down the stairs.

"Oh, there you are!" the chaperone said, her voice sprightly. "We were wondering whether we would have to wait for you."

"We've been here for at least three minutes," Joan told her, laughing.

"I hope you had an enjoyable time," Miss Duncan said as they filed out of the hotel to the quaint, bustling street. "I certainly wouldn't want you to go home and say that you found Belgium boring."

The girls glanced at one another. Joan's eyes were dancing.

"I can't say that we've found Belgium exactly boring, can you, Felicia?"

They crossed the street and took a cab to the museum.

"I had a phone call from Miss Anderson this morning," the teacher announced. "She wanted to remind us that they are having church every night this week."

Dot Craig groaned. "You don't mean that we're going to have to go to church again, do you?" she exclaimed.

"I don't think it would particularly hurt you, Dorothy," Miss Duncan said, "or any of the rest of us for that matter."

"I know, but twice in one week! That's too much!"

Felicia felt the box, bulging conspicuously in her pocket. "I'd like to go tonight," she said.

"So would I," Joan added.

Miss Duncan looked over at Linda and Dot. "I found the service last night most intriguing."

They went out to the little church that evening, arriving a few minutes before the service was to begin, and sat on one side about halfway down.

Felicia Cartright's pulse was fast and irregular, and every fiber in her being tingled nervously. The little building was about half filled. She began to study the somber faces.

Was it the little bald-headed man in front of her? Or the shaggy-browed student with piercing black eyes and a gaunt, hungry look? Or could it be the matronly, gray-haired grandmother whose coat was threadbare?

"Dear God," she prayed silently, almost wordlessly, "help me to get rid of this diamond tonight. Help me to get it to the one who's supposed to have it!"

Jean Anderson came in and waved to them.

This evening it was a little easier to follow the message. The pastor spoke as rapidly as before, but they were more used to him now.

Halfway through the simple, hard-hitting message, Dot leaned over and whispered in Linda's ear.

"Did you ever listen to anyone who could make you feel so miserable?" she asked.

Linda shook her head. She had been trying, desperately, to keep her mind off the message. But she could not. It knifed through her complacency and laid her heart wide open with deft, sure strokes. Grimly she steeled herself against the power of the message.

At last, it was over. She sighed deeply. She had gotten through another message without yielding.

Felicia began to fidget as they sang the last song. This time she had to make contact. She had to get rid of that lacquered box and its precious contents.

The instant the benediction was over Jean started

back to them, but Felicia turned and hurried toward the door.

She made it before Jean reached her and, crossing the foyer, stepped out into the dark, foggy night. She rushed down the steps and stopped. But no one was there!

Her heart sank within her.

Her contact should have met her. The note indicated as much. But the whole sidewalk on that side of the street was empty.

CHAPTER 8

A THIRD MESSAGE

Felicia stood for a long minute on the steps, looking first one direction and then the other. Finally, she turned and went back into the church.

Joan was waiting for her just inside.

"Did you find him?" she asked, her lips only forming the words.

Felicia shook her head.

Miss Duncan and the other two girls were standing in the foyer talking to Jean Anderson.

"The message tonight was so challenging," the young missionary was saying. "I'm so glad that you could come."

"So am I," Miss Duncan replied.

Dot Craig wrinkled her nose distastefully.

"Know something?" Joan broke in. "I'm starved. Are there any good places to eat around here?"

"There's a lovely little place not too far from here,"

Jean said, "but I don't know whether I could direct you there or not."

"Won't you join us?" Miss Duncan asked. "We'd love to have you."

Jean Anderson guided them along one narrow street, across to another, and finally into a cheery, little place that the average tourist never found.

They ordered and sat around the table, chatting merrily.

"If you'll pardon my saying so," Linda began, turning to Jean, "there's something I find very strange about you."

She smiled.

"And what's that?"

"I can't get over the fact that you're a missionary. You seem so sure of yourself. So happy."

"The happiest people I've ever met have been missionaries," she answered. "There's something about being in the center of the Lord's will that brings happiness that the world knows nothing about. And very few go out as missionaries unless they are in the Lord's will."

Linda watched her wistfully. "That must be what the minister was talking about this evening."

"Not exactly," Jean answered. "He was talking about sin and putting your trust in Jesus Christ for salvation. That, of course, is the first thing. It has to come before we can even think about doing God's will."

"Sin!" Dot spoke contemptuously. "I don't know why every preacher has to spend so much time talking about sin. This matter of being in the Lord's will and living the way He wants me to is appealing to me, but when you mention that to a Christian, he starts to talk to you about sin. I don't see what that's got to do with it."

"The Bible says, *All have sinned, and come short of the glory of God*," Felicia put in.

"And in another place," Jean said, "God tells us, *The wages of sin is death; but the gift of God is eternal life.* That means we can't consider anything regarding our relationship to God until we have met and answered the sin question."

"What did you do?" Dot asked, her lips curling bitterly. "Bring us here so you could preach to us?" Her eyes were wide and staring.

Miss Duncan laid a hand on Dorothy's arm, tenderly.

"We have been praying for you," she said. "That you would settle the sin question in your life and put your trust in Christ as Savior."

For a moment Dot stared from one to another. Then she pushed back from the table noisily.

"I don't care what you do," she retorted, near tears, "but I've got a frightful headache. I'm going back to the hotel."

Miss Duncan got up too. "I'll go with you, Dorothy," she said.

Linda rose too. "I think I'd better go," she said quickly, as though she was afraid to remain with Felicia, Joan, and Jean.

"You girls can remain, if you wish, Felicia," Miss Duncan said. "If you have trouble finding the hotel, you can always take a cab."

No one spoke until after the others were gone.

"I wish they would have stayed," Joan said. "That was the first time I've seen real concern in Dot. She's always been so hard, so indifferent before."

Felicia nodded.

They ate slowly, talking with their new friend endlessly. They were still talking when the waiter came up to Felicia and bowed respectfully.

"Pardon, Mademoiselle," he said, "the gentleman at the door handed me this note to give to you."

She looked up, startled. "But I don't know anyone here," she began.

There was no one at the door, and when she turned back to the waiter to question him, he was gone. The note lay on the table at her elbow.

"You must have an admirer, Felicia," Jean told her. "I've been here for almost a year and nothing like that has happened to me."

But the Cartright girl scarcely heard her.

"The handwriting is the same, Joan," she said, her voice hushed and tense.

"Aren't you going to open it?"

Felicia glanced around uncertainly. "I–I don't think I dare," she said.

"But what if he wants to make contact now?"

"I hadn't thought of that." She opened the envelope carefully and read the note inside.

"Don't keep me in suspense like this," Joan countered. "What does it say?"

Felicia lowered her voice to a whisper.

"Tomorrow," she read, "Same place. Same time." Her hand was trembling as she folded the note and put it into her purse. "I don't know why it couldn't have been tonight," she said. "I'm liking this less all the time."

For a long minute, silence enveloped them.

"I don't mean to be prying," Jean said sincerely, "but you are in trouble, aren't you?"

Joan nodded. "We're into something up to our ears," she said. "And the worst of it is that we don't know what it's all about."

The missionary sipped her tea.

"Would you care to tell me about it?" she asked.

"We couldn't tell you here," Felicia countered. "We'd have to go to a place where we'd be sure we weren't overheard."

"My apartment is only two or three blocks from here."

They finished eating, paid their checks, and went out into the foggy, night air. They said nothing until they reached the big, stone house where Jean lived with other missionaries.

"Now," she said, "I don't think you'll be overheard by anyone who would do you harm."

Felicia sighed. "You may not believe this," she began, "but the story is true. Every word of it."

Jean said nothing until the Cartright girl finished.

"That is amazing," she said at last. "It's one of the most amazing things I've ever heard."

"If only we had made contact last night," Joan said, "all of this would be over and done with."

"Would you like to see what's causing all the trouble?" Felicia asked, taking the box from her coat pocket.

"If you aren't violating a confidence in showing it to me."

"We aren't violating any more of a confidence in doing that than we've violated already," Joan said. "But we had to have someone to talk with."

Felicia unwrapped the lacquered box carefully and started to hand it to Jean. It slipped from her fingers!

The uncut diamond spilled from the box and bounced on the granite hearthstone.

"Look!" Joan cried.

The stone split in two!

CHAPTER 9

CORNERED

Felicia Cartright's lithe body stiffened. Her head swam, and her forehead pearled with perspiration. She took half a step forward, almost involuntarily.

"I–I've ruined it!" she exclaimed. "I've ruined the diamond!"

Joan stopped and picked up the pieces.

"I'm terribly sorry," Jean Anderson told her. "I didn't realize that you were going to let go of it."

"The fault was mine."

While the others talked, Joan Bailey turned the pieces, thoughtfully, in her hands.

"I always thought a diamond was hard," she said.

"It's the hardest known gem," Felicia said, "according to the textbook on minerals we have at school."

"I thought I remembered that much of geology." Joan's full lips pursed. "Then why did it crack this way? It was only dropped. It wasn't even thrown hard."

Jean looked over her shoulder.

"Do you suppose it's actually a diamond?"

"I don't know how to tell," Felicia said, taking a piece from her friend and turning it between thumb and forefinger, "but it doesn't look like glass."

"It might be some other kind of gem; something that isn't so hard."

"Or," the Cartright girl suggested, "it might be a diamond with a crack in it or what they call a fracture."

Jean took the piece from Felicia and, moving over to the light, looked at it critically.

"It does look something like a diamond," she said, "but if it is, you're probably right about the crack. It must have been there already."

"But the Duvalls told us that it was worth a great deal of money," Felicia countered, "and if it was cracked, it wouldn't be, would it?"

"A diamond cutter I met at church was telling me that stones like that are worth only a fraction of what a sound, flawless stone would bring," Jean said.

"Of course, there's always a chance that neither the Duvalls nor Wolejeski knew he had a fractured diamond," Joan said.

Felicia sighed deeply. "And tomorrow night I've got to meet Wolejeski's cousin and give him a broken diamond."

"They would have had to find out about the stone sooner or later," the missionary said. "After all, it isn't your fault the gem has a flaw."

"I know." She put the pieces back into the box and returned it to her pocket. "But so very much depends upon it."

"I suppose we'd better go," Joan said. "If we don't show up at a reasonable time, Miss Duncan will be worried."

They went to the door. Felicia was about to open it when Joan put a hand on her arm.

"Wait!"

Shivers ran up the Cartright girl's spine.

"S-s-somebody's out there," Joan said, stammering.

"What do you mean?"

"Somebody's watching the house. I caught a glimpse of him just a minute ago. He's standing by those bushes."

"Are you sure?"

"I'm sure enough so that I'm not going out there," Joan exclaimed. "That's one thing."

"What are we going to do?" Felicia asked.

"We could call Miss Duncan and stay here all night."

Felicia thought for a moment. "Is there a back door?" she asked. "It may be that he thinks we don't know he's out there. If that's true, we could sneak out the back door, and he'd never be the wiser."

"Our back door leads to the alley," Jean told them. "Unless he has someone in the back watching, he'll never know that you're gone."

"You make it sound so easy," Joan replied.

"We'd better hurry," the Cartright girl said. "The longer we stay here, the sooner he's apt to get suspicious and start looking around."

They followed the young missionary in the darkness through the long, narrow hall to the back door.

At the door, she stopped. "I'll be praying for you," she told them.

"We appreciate that."

Felicia put her hand forward to open the door.

"If that guy out there catches us," her companion whispered, "and finds the diamond, he's apt to dump us in the nearest river so we won't tell on him."

She caught her breath. "Do you suppose that would make a difference?" She paused uncertainly.

"I have it," Jean exclaimed. "You girls can take our coats and leave yours here. You can leave the stone too. That way, if he does see you, the chances are he'll think you're someone else. And if he stops and searches you, he won't find anything."

She disappeared in the darkness. Moments later she returned with two heavy coats of Belgian cut.

"He'll be watching for two Americans," she said. "He'll never even recognize you."

Joan wriggled into the coat that was two sizes too large. "In fact," she said, snickering, "I don't think he'll even be able to find me in here."

Fighting the fear that welled within them, they opened the door and slipped silently out into the night.

"Felicia," Joan whispered, "it's dark out here."

"For once I'm glad that it is."

"Do–do you know which way to go?"

"If we ever find our way out of this alley, I do," she answered.

They half expected someone to sneak up behind them as they crept stealthily up the alley and turned out into the street.

"Well," Joan said, expelling her breath with a sigh, "I guess he didn't see us after all."

"Now if we can get to the hotel without being seen," Felicia answered.

It wasn't far to the hotel, but it seemed to take hours to reach it. They were both panting heavily when they reached the empty lobby. The clerk, nodding sleepily, didn't even see them come in.

"I'm glad no one saw us come in," Joan whispered on the steps.

"You can say that again! Right now, all I want to do is lock ourselves in our room and put my head under the pillow and try to go to sleep."

The light in the hall that led to their room was out. Felicia took the key from her pocket and began to fumble along the hall.

"Here's our door," Joan said softly.

"Are you sure?"

"Try the key and we'll find out."

They opened the door and stepped inside. Joan turned to feel for the light switch.

"Don't turn on the light," a thin, rasping voice whispered.

Joan jumped back and threw her hands to her mouth. A weak, strangled scream escaped her lips.

"Mademoiselle," a man ordered sternly, "don't do that again!"

"Who are you?" Felicia insisted, surprisingly calm. "And what do you want?"

"Close the door." The voice was soft and faintly familiar, in spite of the accent. "Close the door."

She did so mechanically.

By this time their eyes had grown accustomed to the darkness. There were others in the room; dark, formless shapes. Felicia counted three of them sitting on chairs, and two others standing behind them.

"Young man!" A familiar voice broke in authoritatively, "I don't want to have to tell you again. This is illegal and highly improper. I must insist that you release us at once."

"Miss Duncan!" Felicia cried. "What are you doing here?"

"That," she retorted crisply, "is something I have been trying to discover for the past hour. This thoroughly obnoxious, young man and his uncouth companions came bursting into our rooms and forced us to come here at the point of a gun."

"A-a-and I'm scared," Dot whimpered.

"You have no need to be frightened, Dorothy," Miss Duncan continued. "These gentlemen, and I use the term loosely, do not dare harm us. We're American citizens and subject to the protection of our flag."

"Mademoiselle," the intruder snapped irritably, "I have been trying to tell you that all you've got to worry about is doing exactly as you're told and nobody's going to get hurt."

"If you were a girl and in one of our classes at Wellington, I would deny you privileges for a month, young man, just for the insolence in your voice."

He sighed his disgust.

"My business is not with you, Mademoiselle." He turned to Felicia and spoke in French. "I believe that you were asking me a question the last time we met," he said, "and I was about to say, 'I would have enjoyed it much better in English.'"

Perspiration broke out on Felicia's forehead, and she felt her throat constrict.

"You're Wolejeski's cousin!"

He ignored her statement. "I've waited far too long already. I'll take the little, black lacquered box now. Quickly! And you can all go back to bed."

"But I–I left it with a friend for safekeeping," she said hesitantly. "We were being followed."

"You left it with someone!" His voice broke angrily. "Your instructions were to keep that box on your person always!"

"Felicia!" Miss Duncan broke in, her voice stern. "I insist on knowing what relationship there is between yourself and these unsavory characters."

"Don't pay any attention to her! Where's that box? And why did you trust it to someone else?" His voice was iced with rage.

"We thought it was the thing to do," Joan said, suddenly finding voice. "We were afraid the guy who was following us would take it away from us."

"You didn't think we wouldn't follow you, do you?" he asked. "Now out with it. Where's that box?"

"It's safe enough," Felicia assured him. "We can have it back here within an hour."

"It had better be safe," he said ominously. "That's all I can tell you!"

"Felicia, I am disappointed in you," Miss Duncan said. "I am terribly disappointed in you. Your choice of friends is appalling."

"Lady," the man with the gun exclaimed bitterly, "I've had about all I can take from you. Keep that trap of yours shut, or I'm going to gag you."

"I must tell you about the diamond," the Cartright girl blurted. "It–"

"Never mind the diamond! I want that box. And I want it now! Tonight!"

"As we said," Joan said, "we can get it and have it back here within an hour."

The silence was deafening.

"I'll give you exactly half an hour to have that box back here in your room!" His voice was harsh and as sharp as the cutting edge of tempered steel.

"And to make sure you get it and bring it to me, I'm going to keep your friends here until you get back!"

Felicia's knees went weak. "I don't know whether I can make it in half an hour or not."

"If you value your friends' lives, you'd better!"

Silence hung over the group.

"And you had better not go near the police!"

CHAPTER 10

THE SECRET COMPARTMENT

A full minute passed, and no one in the quiet little room spoke. The stranger glanced at his watch.

"Your half hour has already begun."

Joan took hold of Felicia's hand. "Come on," she said softly, "we've got to hurry."

The two girls turned and went down the stairs and through the lobby numbly.

"F-Felicia," Joan whispered in her companion's ear, "I don't like this at all."

"Neither do I," the Cartright girl answered.

"The police station is only two or three blocks down the street."

"We don't dare!" Felicia protested. "They'll have us followed! We wouldn't even get to the door of the police station before they would know. And they've still got Miss Duncan and the girls." She took a deep breath and exhaled wearily. "No, we don't dare go to the police."

"What can we do, then?"

"First of all, we'll go straight to Jean's and pick up that box," Felicia informed her.

Joan glanced over her shoulder. "I think you're right about someone following us," she said. "I just saw a man in a dark coat crossing the street about half a block back."

They walked as rapidly as they could to the big, stone mansion where Jean Anderson had an apartment.

"She's still up," Joan exclaimed, seeing the light in the living room.

They ran up the stairs and knocked on the door.

"Quick!" Felicia whispered when Jean answered their knock. "Let us in and close the door."

"What's the matter?" she wanted to know. "Has something happened?"

"You can say that again," Joan said, "and twice on Saturday."

Tensely, Felicia told her what had happened. "And they're holding Miss Duncan and the girls as hostages until we get back with the box. So we've got to hurry!"

"That's strange," Jean said, her brow furrowing. "According to the Duvalls, you were only to be concerned with getting the diamond into the hands of this man. Now all he cares about is the box. I don't understand it."

"Neither do I."

"Unless," Joan volunteered, "they wanted to deceive us into thinking they were concerned about getting the diamond into Antwerp when all the time it's the box that's valuable."

"But I don't see why they would do that," Felicia countered.

"Neither do I," her companion answered, "but it would explain why the diamond broke when you dropped it. They could have bought a cheap stone just to deceive us."

Felicia thought momentarily. "I suppose that could be right. But I still can't understand why. Do you suppose this whole story about Wolejeski is a lie?"

Joan pursed her lips. "I can tell you this much. We're into something that's a whole lot bigger than getting one man to the West."

Jean left the room and, in a moment, came back with the box. "I don't understand it either," she said, "but here it is."

"It's only an ordinary looking box, isn't it?" Felicia said.

"When I was a little girl," Jean continued, "my aunt, who is a missionary to Japan, brought me a box like that when she came home on furlough. It intrigued me because–" She stopped speaking and began to examine the box carefully. "This one is almost like the one she brought me, only this is much more expensive and intricate."

Neither Joan nor Felicia spoke.

Jean continued to work with it.

"See!" she exclaimed. "There's a secret compartment here! Just as I thought!"

With that she opened a secret drawer in the black box.

Felicia's eyes widened. "All the times I handled it I didn't once suspect that was there."

"There must be something in this compartment that would make those guys want this box."

"It looks empty to me," the Cartright girl answered.

"Maybe there's another compartment," Joan suggested. "If there's one, there could be another one."

"No," Felicia answered, "there isn't room."

She took the small drawer out of the box and squinted into the opening.

"Girls!" she cried. "Look here!" With a bobby pin, she loosened a neat roll of paper from its hiding place behind the drawer.

"What is it?" Joan demanded.

For answer Felicia began to unfold the tissue-thin paper.

"It's a drawing," she said. "It must be plans of some sort."

Joan bent over her shoulder and was reading thoughtfully. "Do you know what this is?" she demanded. "These are the plans for a missile launcher on a nuclear submarine!" She pointed to the legend at the bottom of the drawing. "It gives everything!

The size, aiming and launching mechanisms; even details for arming the atomic warhead in the missile!"

Jean Anderson's face was ashen. Felicia suddenly went limp.

"But why would anyone want information like this?" she asked. "Who would get any good from it?"

"There's only one nation it would help," Joan said, her voice numb as the realization came to her.

"Russia!" Felicia spat out the word.

"And they've got the spy system to get information like this!"

"That means the Duvalls, the man in customs who let me through without searching me or putting the diamond on my declaration sheet, and the guys who are holding Miss Duncan and the girls are all Communist agents!" She gulped hard.

"What are we going to do?"

"We can't take these papers back to the hotel," the Cartright girl said. "Not even with Miss Duncan and the others in danger. Information like this is too harmful to the United States."

"We can slip out the back way," Jean said, "and go across the alley. The people over there will be better able to contact the police." She turned and took her coat from the closet. "I'll go with you."

"Do you think we can convince the police that our story is true?" Felicia asked.

"We've got to." Joan spoke with grim determination.

It was dark in the long hallway, but they did not

dare turn on the lights. Felicia, going first, felt her way along the strange, musty passageway and down the wide marble steps.

Jean and the Bailey girl were right behind her.

"Here's a door," Felicia whispered. "Does it lead outside?"

"Out into a little courtyard," Jean said. "Be careful when you open it. Sometimes it squeaks."

Breathing a prayer, Felicia turned the knob stealthily and eased the door open. It moved silently.

"Come on," she whispered. "I think the way is clear."

At that very instant, rough hands snatched at her.

"Let go of me!" she screamed, struggling to free herself.

But the stranger's grip tightened on her left arm, and his other hand clamped firmly over her mouth.

Joan and the missionary girl turned to flee, but a towering brute of a man emerged from the shadows, silently, and grabbed them both.

Joan began to scream.

"Stop that," he muttered, cursing, "or none of you will live to see tomorrow! Now give me that box!"

It wasn't until then that Felicia recognized the voice as belonging to the man who had waited for them in their room.

"Give me that box," he repeated. "And be quick about it!"

"It's in my pocket," Felicia told him. "Take it yourself!"

He jerked the little lacquered box from her pocket and gave her a shove toward the alley.

"You'd have saved yourself a lot of trouble if you had given it to me in the first place. Now keep moving. All three of you. And don't try any funny stuff if you don't want to get hurt!"

They were shoved along the dark alley to the street where two small black cars were waiting, one behind the other. The men guided them to the first.

"Now get in there," the spokesman hissed, "and be quick about it."

"What are you going to do with us?" Joan demanded.

"And what have you done to Miss Duncan and the other girls?"

He laughed and closed the car door. An instant later he got in and began to slowly drive away.

CHAPTER 11

IN COMMUNIST HANDS

For several minutes, Felicia, Joan, and the youthful missionary did not move. The car was still traveling through the streets of Antwerp at a reasonable speed.

"Felicia," Joan whispered, "can you reach the door handle?"

She moved cautiously. "I think so."

"When I count three, open the door, and we'll all jump."

"Stop that whispering!" a harsh voice ordered from the front seat.

No one answered him. For a time, even Joan was silent.

"Okay?" she mouthed at last.

Cautiously Felicia reached for the handle.

"Oh, no, you don't!" The front-seat passenger rapped her knuckles with his fist so sharply that she cried out in spite of herself. "Behave yourselves, and no harm'll come to you. But if you try that stuff, you're just asking for trouble!"

"What are we going to do with them?" the driver asked under his breath.

"You tend to your driving and leave the thinking to me."

The guy kept a close watch as his companion drove. Felicia settled back in the seat.

"Now you're making sense," he told her.

How far they drove, the girls did not know. They went through one narrow, twisting street after another; past a row of musty apartment buildings and a section of small shops. They must have turned onto a highway after a time, for the driver began to pick up speed. And Felicia noticed that the road had widened considerably.

The man in the front seat had turned until he was almost facing them. Even in the semidarkness, they could see the brutal cut to his jaw, the fire in his beady, black eyes.

Joan, who was sitting in the middle, leaned forward and peered out the window with studied carelessness. If only she could make out a familiar building or spot a street sign.

"You can quit looking, Mademoiselle," their captor told her, laughing shortly. "You will see nothing along here that will tell you where you are or where we're going to take you."

Felicia Cartright bowed her head and began to pray silently. The young missionary was doing the same. Joan followed suit.

"Our Father and our God," she began, "we know that You know all things and that You watch over us and care for us. Tonight, we are putting our trust in You. . . ."

As they prayed, their hearts began to be still, and they could think again.

The man in the front seat put the window down two or three inches and turned his attention toward the far horizon. They were out in the country now and not too far from the ocean. The girls could taste the salt in the air.

The first faint, gray streaks of dawn were tracing patterns of light across the coast as they pulled up before a great, towering castle on the sea. It was an ancient, medieval fortress, built by some long-forgotten king.

The driver stopped and both men jumped out.

"Now get out of this car," the spokesman said, his voice ominously quiet. "And don't try anything. See?"

"You won't need to worry about us," Joan told him. "We–we're not going to give you any trouble out here."

"You can just bet you're not."

By that time, a second car had pulled up behind them.

"Miss Duncan!" Felicia cried.

"I am going to learn the meaning of this," Miss Duncan was saying as the car door was jerked open. Her lips were cold and firm in her best "Dean-of-Women manner." "We are American citizens. I demand that you unhand us immediately and take steps to see that transportation back to our hotel is provided us."

"Oh, stop gabbing, and do as I tell you!" the man snapped irritably.

Miss Duncan got out of the car with careful deliberation. Dot and Linda followed. The girls were white and shaken. Goose bumps stood out on their arms.

"Get your coats, girls," Miss Duncan said to them. "You'll catch your death."

"I said, Get moving."

"And I, young man," Miss Duncan announced, turning to fix a withering stare on him, "told them to get their coats."

"All right. All right. But be quick about it."

The four men herded Miss Duncan and the girls up the worn steps and into the hallway.

"Now," the leader exclaimed fervently, "we'll know where you are when we want you."

"What are we going to do with them?" one of the men asked again.

The spokesman did not answer him. Instead, he turned his back and began to work with the little lacquered box. Joan's gaze caught Felicia's. She winked slowly.

When the guy turned back to them, his face was livid. "All right," he said, snarling. "This is no time for games. Where are those papers?"

"We thought you wanted the box," Joan answered. "At least that's what you told us."

"What did you do with them?"

"With what?" the Bailey girl asked him.

"You know what I'm talking about!" His voice rose to a shout. "Give me those papers, and be quick about it!"

"First the Duvalls asked us to deliver a diamond to Antwerp. Then you came to us and didn't care about the diamond. You wanted the box. Now you don't want the box; you want some sort of papers." Joan's eyes widened innocently. "Are you sure you know what you want?"

"Mademoiselle," he cried, "it is well for you that I am a patient man! Now what did you do with those papers?"

"Suppose you find out," she retorted defiantly.

"Let me work her over, boss," a big, gorilla-like thug put in. "I can make her talk. Just let me twist her arm. She'll tell us all she knows."

"I'll have you know that I shall hold *you* personally responsible for this outrage!" Miss Duncan snapped, pushing close to the spokesman. "You are dealing with citizens of the United States of America! Don't you forget it."

"Shut up! All of you!" The man was trembling

with rage and frustration. He turned to his hench-men. "Take them up to the tower room. I've got to contact M'sieu X!"

"Okay, boss, but I still think you ought to let me make her talk." He grabbed Joan and Felicia roughly by the arms and shoved them ahead of him toward the stairs. "Now the rest of you had better come along and not give me any trouble. I'm not as soft and easy as *he* is."

The six of them marched silently up first one staircase and then another.

"I want you to notice the construction of this edifice," Miss Duncan said as they climbed. "The windows are tall and narrow. Can you give me the name for this type of construction, Dorothy?"

"G-g-gothic?"

"That is correct."

Joan snickered.

"Miss Duncan is trying to educate us on the way to the gallows," she whispered in Felicia's ear.

"I want you to take particular notice of the drapes," the chaperone said. "Do you notice anything unusual about them?"

"They look as though they haven't been dusted for a hundred years," Felicia observed. She looked over at Linda and Dot. Their faces were tight and drawn, and fear flickered in their eyes. To be honest, she didn't feel so well herself.

At last they reached the tower, and their captor thrust them inside.

"Now," he snarled, "do you want to give me that paper, or do I beat it out of you?"

"Whatever it is," Miss Duncan snapped, "don't give it to them."

The huge ruffian made them empty their purses and take off their shoes.

"Now that's better," he exclaimed triumphantly as he spotted the thin roll of paper Felicia had stuck so hastily into her left shoe.

She glowered at him.

He snatched the paper and unrolled it hurriedly. "The Duvalls are going to be very happy to learn that their courier got through safely."

"I wasn't their courier!" Felicia informed him hotly.

The man chuckled.

"You served just as well as though you were a loyal party member." His grin was wide. "To tell you the truth, you did a better job than we could have done ourselves. Especially with the authorities watching the Duvall farm the way they did after Jardien broke under questioning and told them where he had sent the courier with the papers." He leaned forward. "Would you believe it? Two days before you arrived, the French Secret Service turned that little farm upside down and couldn't find a thing." He laughed again, deeply. "Old Duvall had hidden them in the well."

"Then it was the police who questioned us," Joan broke in.

"Miss Cartright," the Wellington Dean of Women said sternly, addressing them the way she did girls who were called before her to be disciplined, "and Miss Bailey, I believe you owe me a complete and thorough explanation. Something has been going on here."

"You can say that again," Joan muttered softly.

"You asked about the police, Mademoiselle," the big man continued. "*Oui,* it was the police." He was chuckling to himself. "But they think only to check you as you come. They think perhaps you might be the ones who bring the papers to M'sieu Duvall and his good wife. They do not know that you come to take them away."

From somewhere below, the other Communist called up to him loudly, authoritatively.

"Hurry up! I can't wait for you all day!"

"I'm coming!" He tucked the paper in his own shoe and straightened to glare at them. "Don't you breathe a word to Maurice that I have the papers, or it will go hard with you. I will give them to M'sieu X myself! I will show him who is the most valuable, the most loyal comrade!"

With that he locked the door and was gone.

No one moved until his footsteps died away. Then Dot began to whimper.

"What's going to happen to us?" she asked, her

voice trembling. "What are they going to do with us now?"

"T-t-that's what I've been wondering," Linda said.

"Girls," Miss Duncan said sharply, "there is no time for whimpering. We are in what Joan would vulgarly call a jam."

She turned to Felicia. "And now," she continued, "suppose you start at the very beginning and tell us what has brought this on."

When she finished, Miss Duncan's eyes were twinkling. "I wish you had taken us into your confidence, don't you, girls? There might have been something we could have done."

Felicia shook her head miserably.

"They've got the papers now," she said, her voice dull and lifeless. "And Joan and I brought them. We've helped betray our country."

Miss Duncan pursed her lips.

"I wouldn't say that it was all over yet," she said firmly.

CHAPTER 12

ESCAPE AND RESCUE

The sun was up now, glistening on the placid sea. Felicia walked over to the narrow window and looked out.

"Did you notice all the boats?" she asked. "We must not be too far from Antwerp."

"You couldn't prove that by me," Joan said. "I thought they drove far enough to have taken us across Europe."

"I heard one of the men in our car mention a submarine on the way out here," Miss Duncan said. "Do you suppose this Monsieur X is coming from the sea?"

"Either that," Joan retorted, her face grim, "or they are going to take us to him by submarine."

"Oh, no!" Dot cried, her hand flying to her mouth. The color ebbed from her cheeks, and terror, stark and full, stood in her eyes.

"Now, Dorothy," Miss Duncan said, "you must not lose control of yourself. We've got to think, girls. Think."

"But I'm scared."

"S-s-so am I," Linda managed, her teeth chattering.

Felicia sat on a narrow plank bench and took her little Bible from her pocket and began to read.

> *Let not your heart be troubled: you believe in God, believe also in me. In my Father's house are many mansions . . .*

As she read, Dot and Linda calmed a little.

"Does that apply to all of us?" Linda asked.

Felicia shook her head. "The Bible says that salvation is for those who have confessed their sin and put their trust in the Savior."

"But I'm good enough," Linda answered.

"And so am I," Dot said. "We don't drink or smoke or cheat or–"

"The Bible says that *all have sinned, and come short of the glory of God*," Felicia said. "And it tells us in another place that *the wages of sin is death; but the gift of God is eternal life.*"

They eyed her quizzically.

"Did you ever envy anyone's grades or clothes or position at school?" Joan asked.

"I suppose so," Dot admitted.

"Have you ever been angry with anyone?"

"I usually make up," she said defensively.

"Have you ever told anyone you had a headache when you didn't have so you could get out of doing something you didn't want to do?"

"But those are such *little* things."

"That's another thing that the Bible teaches," Joan continued. "There just aren't any little sins. If we break part of the law, we've broken all of it. That's why Jesus Christ had to come down to earth and die on the cross. Because none of us, regardless of how good we are, can hope to live up to the law. So the only way for you or me or anyone to be saved is to believe what Jesus Christ says."

Dot and Linda swallowed hard. "You make us feel so miserable."

"It isn't Joan or I who's making you feel miserable," Felicia said. "It's the Holy Spirit. He's speaking to your hearts."

They shifted uneasily.

"I felt the same way you do right now," Joan said gently, "and I kept on feeling that way until I confessed my sin and accepted Christ."

Linda and Dot looked at one another questioningly.

"I will if you will," Linda said at last.

Her friend nodded.

They all bowed their heads reverently and began to pray.

It was sometime later when they looked up. For

two or three minutes they sat around, not saying much. Dorothy and Linda smiled wanly.

"I don't feel very different," Linda said.

"But you are different," Jean Anderson assured her. "You have been born again. You're saved. That's the important thing."

The others remained seated, but Joan got to her feet and began to examine the room carefully.

"There's got to be something we can do to get out of here," she said. "And quickly! Before they get those papers to that M'sieu X, whoever he is."

The lower floor of the old castle may have been wired for electricity, but current had never been brought up to the tower room. There was no light at all, except for a long candle on a shelf.

"At least they were thoughtful enough to provide us with light," Joan said, holding it up.

"I should rather think that former occupants left it," Miss Duncan said. "I'm sure our friends wouldn't care whether we sat here in the dark or not."

"Do any of you have a mirror?" the Bailey girl asked. "I think I've got an idea."

Miss Duncan opened her purse. "I have a mirror," she said, "but I cannot understand your wanting to check your makeup at a time like this."

They all laughed.

"As a matter of fact, Joan," Miss Duncan said, "I thought of signaling by mirror, but these windows are too small to allow us to catch the rays of the sun."

"That isn't exactly what I had in mind."

The hours passed endlessly. Felicia marked the coming of noon and the march of the sun across the horizon by noting the shadows through the windows.

"What do you suppose they're waiting for?" Jean Anderson asked.

"I'm afraid they're waiting for darkness," Miss Duncan said calmly.

"Do you suppose they are planning on taking us out to sea?" Dot asked.

"Dorothy," the chaperone spoke quietly, "we are not to think of what they may or may not do. We have all prayed, asking God's guidance. Now we must put our trust in Him."

The girl smiled. "Twenty-four hours ago, if anyone would have told me I'd be calm in a situation like this, I'd have thought they were off their rocker."

At last, darkness came.

There were still boats out in the channel. They could see the lights winking merrily.

"Joan," Miss Duncan said suddenly, "if you have a plan of action, I think it would be wise to start now. In other words, 'time's a-wastin.'"

"I'm way ahead of you," the Bailey girl said. Hurriedly, she broke the candle into several short pieces, mounted them together on a small board, and lighted them with a match she found on the shelf.

"Now give me the mirror, Felicia."

Her companion picked up the mirror and held it behind the candles.

"I had a brother who was a boy scout," Joan mumbled. "I don't know what he learned, but I learned this much of the Morse code."

"SOS," she flashed. SOS. . . SOS . . . SOS . . . The girls gathered around her tensely, prayerfully. She had been signaling for almost five minutes when they heard the sound of feet running frantically up the stairs.

"They're coming!" Linda cried in a harsh whisper. "They're coming!"

"What are we going to do?"

"Keep right on, Joan and Felicia," Miss Duncan ordered. "We'll take care of our captors."

Saying this, she clambered up on the bench, jerked the heavy, dust-laden drapes until they came down, and turned toward the door.

"When he comes in, make a dive for his feet!" By that time one of their captors was at the door. "You in there!" he cried, fumbling with the key. "What are you trying to do? Stop that or we'll stop you!"

Miss Duncan gathered the drapes in her arms and tiptoed along the bench until she reached the door.

"Now remember," she whispered, "when he comes in, be sure and dive for his feet."

"But what–?"

At that moment, the door swung open, and their angered captor burst in.

Miss Duncan, standing on tiptoes, threw the dusty drapes over his head, and then, in one swift motion, wrapped them around his arms.

"W–," he choked.

A split second later, the girls swarmed at his legs. He fell to the floor, coughing violently.

"Hold him still!" Miss Duncan puffed. "Hold him!" She jerked off his shoe, retrieved the papers, and tied one drape around his legs. "Come, girls! Quickly!"

She scrambled for the door, locked it, and the five girls followed her.

"We've got to get out of here!" the chaperone exclaimed.

They went plunging down the steep stairs and dashed out of the house. For a fraction of time, they stopped in the courtyard.

"This way!" Miss Duncan said, and she led them into the marsh and brush that surrounded the castle.

"I–I think we made it," Joan gasped.

"We can thank God for that," Felicia answered.

"We can thank God He sent us with someone like Miss Duncan too," the Bailey girl said.

"There is no time for eulogy," the Dean of Women told them. "We've got to put as much distance between us and that castle as possible."

They had been making their way through the marsh for some time when they heard a fast launch come roaring toward shore.

"What's that?" Linda asked.

"That is the police launch," the missionary girl told her. "They must have seen our SOS."

* * * *

It was two days later. Miss Duncan and the girls were sitting together in Jean Anderson's apartment.

"They picked up the last of that spy ring this morning," Felicia said. "The Duvalls are in jail in Paris."

"We can be thankful that we got those papers back," Miss Duncan said. "It would have been tragic to have had them fall into enemy hands."

"The authorities seemed almost as glad to have them for evidence," Joan put in. "If it weren't for the papers, they wouldn't have had the evidence they needed to convict the spy ring. I understand that was the reason they hadn't arrested the Duvalls before. They knew they were Communists and had good reason to suppose they were enemy agents, but they couldn't get the evidence for a conviction."

"They won't bother anyone for a long while," Miss Duncan said.

"And just think," Linda said, "when Felicia's Great-Uncle Don talked with them about Jesus Christ, they were at a turning point in their lives. If they had trusted Him as their Savior, they would have been true to their country and ours. And they would have saved themselves all this heartache and punishment."

"I was thinking the same thing," Dot said softly.

"You and I came to a turning point in our lives, too, when we accepted Christ as Savior."

"But we turned the right way."

There was a short silence. "I'm anxious to get home and tell Mom and Dad about the Savior," Dot added.

Miss Duncan got to her feet uneasily.

"Speaking of home," she began, "we'll be there in a few days, and there's one request I'd like to make of you."

"What's that?" they chorused.

"I am afraid I was not too ladylike when I–a–," she coughed nervously, "when I wrapped that unsavory gentleman in the draperies."

"You can say that again," Joan told her, laughing.

"The student body at Wellington might get the wrong impression if they heard about it. And–and after all, I am responsible for the discipline there."

"So you'd like to have us keep quiet about your part in the episode, is that it?" Felicia asked.

Miss Duncan beamed. "You are an understanding girl, Felicia, with a true Wellington spirit."

"You can count on us," Joan broke in brashly. "Mum's the word."

She winked at Miss Duncan slowly, extravagantly.

The solemn-faced Dean of Women winked in return.

THE
FELICIA CARTRIGHT
SERIES

Felicia Cartright, a petite blonde who is one of the most popular students at Wellington School for Girls, has a surprising inclination toward mysteries. If a mysterious situation arises, it either makes its way to Felicia, or Felicia somehow finds it. Though this is a bit trying for her happy-go-lucky roommate, Joan Bailey, it does prevent life from becoming monotonous. It also enables Bernard Palmer, the popular author of the "Danny Orlis" books, to write an entertaining series of stories for girls aged twelve to eighteen.

The mysteries range from a valuable missing antique to an attempt by claim jumpers to steal a deposit of tungsten ore. There's excitement and action galore—but there's also spiritual guidance and blessing because Felicia and her partner-in-adventure love the Lord and take Him into account in all their experiences.

AVAILABLE FROM WWW.ANEKOPRESS.COM